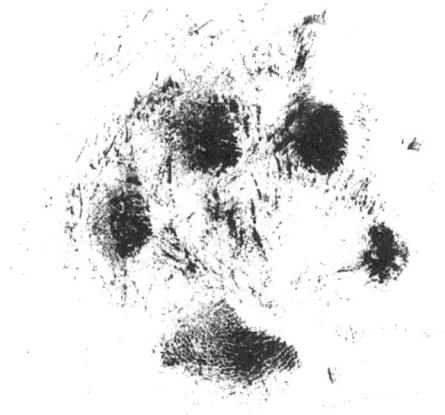

Roo

More Than Just a Dachshund

The Journey Continues

Roo

More Than Just a Dachshund

The Journey Continues

Written by Richard Lentz 🐾 Illustrated by Gary Hovland

HIS Publishing Group
4310 Wiley Post Rd.
Suite 201D
Dallas, TX 75001

HIS Publishing Group is a division of Human Improvement Specialists, llc.
For information visit www.hispubg.com or contact publisher at *info@hispubg.com*

Illustrations and Cover Design by Gary Hovland
Back Cover Image by Becky Miller with Corporate Video Inc.
Becky also assisted Gary Hovland in coordinating the back cover.
Dallas sunset September 2, 2023, by Dallas McNeal of Dallas McNeal Photography.
Coordination with past photographs and research done by
Nancy Davis of Nancy Davis & Associates

ISBN-13: 979-8-218-97580-7

1. Children 2. Life Skills 3. Inspirational

Summary: A continuing story that reflects life's journey through the eyes of a miniature dachshund. Filled with many emotions, trial and tribulations just as people encounter. Provided by the publisher.

10 9 8 7 6 5 4 3 2 1

Dedication

THIS BOOK IS WRITTEN AS A TRIBUTE TO ROO, MY BEST FRIEND. For his entire life, Roo has demonstrated what unconditional love truly means. Roo will never know how many hearts he has touched and smiles he has brought to so many faces. God gives us so many gifts, and we are grateful for all of them, but Roo was simply an angel in the body of a miniature long-haired dachshund. Roo brought Annette and me closer together and made our family whole.

Special Thanks

ANNETTE FOR BEING MY partner and sharing this unbelievable experience called Roo.

Byron and Alice Scarborough, who know the trials and tribulations of life with pets. Thank you for all your support through thick and thin.

Meg Nazworth, D.V.M., for being there for us at our darkest times.

Illustrator Gary Hovland

FOR OVER THIRTY-FIVE YEARS Gary Holand's whimisical pen and ink and water-color illustrations have appeared in the nation's most acclaimed magazines and newpapers, as well as many international publications. He is a graduate of Art Center College of Design in Pasadena, CA., where he later taught an un undergraduate course in "Humorous Illustration". His clients have included Simon and Schuster Publishing, Alfred Knopf Publishing, The New York Times, The New Yorker, Esquire, W, Vanity Fair, The Washington Post, and The Wall Street Journal. He lives in an old house in Louisville, Kentucky.

Hello, everybody

FOR THOSE OF YOU WHO READ MY BOOK, welcome back. For you newcomers, let me introduce myself. My name is Roo. I am a chocolate brindle miniature long-haired dachshund. I wrote a book several years ago, *Life's Little Lessons*, mainly for children. I am picking up where the first book stopped.

I feel like this is a series on Netflix that has been gone for a long time and then picks up from where the show left off. Well, this has been a longer layoff. It's not that I didn't want to stay in touch, but life moves so fast. Sometimes, there is not enough time in the day to do everything you want.

Little Sis

WHEN WE LAST SPOKE, Heidi (my little sister) was getting ready to go to school. I'm not saying she flunked out, but let's just say she didn't excel. What she did learn, she either didn't bother to apply or it just didn't stick.

Heidi is extremely independent. I like to stay close to my peeps because I think that is where the action is. Heidi, on the other paw, tends to do her own thing. She won't wander off too far from us, but she definitely likes her alone time. Pops says Heidi takes after Mom because she is so inquisitive. She is always exploring and checking things out. She has no interest in playing ball or chewing on toys, especially the ones that squeak. Healthwise, Heidi has had more than her share of health issues. For such a small dog, she has had some major setbacks. Her first major problem was with her back. She was jumping up and down while Pops was eating, and he heard a pop. Heidi hid under the table, but Pops immediately knew something was wrong. Heidi could no longer move her back legs. Dachshunds are prone to have back problems due to our long bodies. Mom and Pops took Heidi to the doctor, and he said she needed back surgery. The surgery was successful, but the recovery period was very long. Gradually, Heidi began to start to walk again. She had kind of a "sidewinder" walk because of the surgery. It was a long time before she was able to walk a straight line again. Heidi was very fast when she was young. Even though she didn't like to exert much energy, she could fly when she wanted to run. She doesn't have world-class speed today like she once did, but she definitely can "pick 'em up and lay 'em down" when she needs to.

Next was pancreatitis which led to ongoing stomach issues. Heidi needed to be on a bland diet for a long time. She has digestive problems from time to time, but overall, she is fine now.

Heidi (our medical miracle) had two episodes of opening up her chest. She was exploring in our backyard and evidently sliced her chest open on some metal landscape edging. Pops noticed she had something hanging from her chest, and he thought it might be hair that needed clipping. When he picked her up, the skin on her chest was laying open. Once again, Mom and Pops rushed her to an emergency vet clinic, and they sewed her up. She was heavily bandaged and looked like a partial mummy for several weeks. Once the bandage was removed and she could start exploring again, somehow, someway, she reopened the wound. What was amazing, Heidi never squealed or cried during any of these medical issues. She is one tough sister. I am glad she persevered through everything. Heidi can be very sweet. She licks my face and eyes to clean me up. She truly cares about me. When I go to the vet or somewhere without her, she always thoroughly smells me to find out where I have been or who I have seen. She also has some quirks, like eating my turds. I guess that could be considered the highest form of flattery, but I think it is absolutely disgusting.

In many ways, we are inseparable. Even though she is very independent, she knows I always have her back.

On the Move...Again

SINCE WE LAST SPOKE, we have moved two more times. The first move was a result of Mom wanting more security, so we moved to a gated community. No matter where you are, there are going to be pluses and minuses. Here are some of the pros and cons from my perspective.

<u>Pluses:</u> *Great walking trail around three lakes. There are ducks everywhere. When we first arrived, I wanted to chase the ducks away, but very soon, I just left them alone. This place has a dog park which was enclosed and had a pavilion for the humans to sit and watch the canines play. There are always lots of tennis balls or dog toys to choose from. I like selecting the perfect ball or toy to give to Pops for some high-level fetch action. At the end of our walks along the trail, we would always pass by the guardhouse on the way back home. I could sense that destination from a mile away because the guard on duty would always give Heidi and me a treat. Nothing better than a crunchy treat after a visit to the dog park and a long walk.*

<u>Negatives:</u> *Our home was two story. Normally, that would not be an issue, but it was not ideal for an aging pup. The upstairs had Mom's "retreat," Pops' office and a guest bedroom. I was not able to go up or down the stairs on my own, so I would need to be carried. Heidi would sometimes make it halfway on her own, but she needed help most of the time. Heidi is more independent than me and could stay by herself downstairs. I always want to be next to Mom or Pops because that is where the action is. The exterior had very little space for Heidi and me to play.*

It soon became apparent the second floor was not going to work long term. Mom has great looking legs, but her knees are not the greatest. Lugging Heidi and me up and down the stairs was not safe.

The second move was to a townhome community. Our house is all on one level with the exception of two steps at the front entry, living room and kitchen.

Pluses: *We have an open park area outside our kitchen door where we can roam and play. We have lots of large windows so we can see all the dogwalkers and their pets from inside. There is always a lot of activity outside our windows for great viewing. We have a larger backyard for Heidi and me to play. There are lots of friendly people, huge trees and bunnies. Pops has even trained some of the bunnies to eat out of his hand.*

Negatives: *Those dang steps. I am getting older, and I don't trust managing the two steps.*

Morning Routines:

Pops leaves early to go to work. I mean, really early. His breakfast (he calls it the breakfast of champions) consists of a banana and yogurt (four days a week) and a banana only on Wednesday. He buys a four-cup set of yogurt to help with his digestion, so he goes with the banana only on Wednesday. Pops and I are very disciplined, and we like our routine. Mom thinks he is a little odd with his unwavering discipline, but I get it. Every weekday morning, he saves the last two pieces of banana for Heidi and me. After the banana, I get to lick the yogurt cup, and Heidi licks the spoon. Most mornings, Heidi sets her banana down and licks the yogurt spoon first. Then she eats the banana. Not me, I scarf my banana immediately and move on to the yogurt portion.

Sometimes Heidi has tummy problems in the morning and doesn't feel like eating her banana or yogurt. I feel sorry she does not feel well, but I gladly will eat her banana and yogurt portions. Sometimes she is a little slow coming out for Pops' morning breakfast. On those mornings, Pops will give me something a little extra but take some to Heidi as well. My motto is, "You snooze, you lose," especially when it comes to food. There are mornings where Heidi and I will go get in bed with Mom as she does her morning reading. On these mornings, Pops will bring our banana pieces to us in bed. I am usually perched up on his side of the bed, anxiously awaiting the banana delivery. Aahhh…breakfast in bed. It doesn't get much better! After the banana delivery, Pops goes in and brushes his teeth and comes back with the dachshund calendar picture for that particular day to give to Mom. He kisses her goodbye, gives Heidi a soft pet or rub and does the same for me. He usually tells me to "hold the fort down," since I am the man of the family when he leaves.

Now weekend breakfasts are a different story. On Saturdays and

Sundays, Pops has granola with yogurt and fruit. He likes to read the paper while munching on his bowl of granola. Heidi and I sit quietly waiting until he finishes. We can usually tell when he is getting close when we hear the click of the spoon hitting the bottom of the bowl. Once Pops is finished, he lets me lick the yogurt cup, and Heidi gets to lick the spoon. Don't think Heidi is getting shortchanged here. When she finishes licking the spoon, Pops scoops up any residue on his bowl. Pops is an equal opportunity employer, and his breakfast routine is no different. This process goes on for several minutes. Aahhh…the weekends. What a special treat! Great breakfast and Pops is going to stick around for a while. I love family times like this.

Seeing Our Peeps

HEIDI AND I ARE ALWAYS excited to see our peeps (parents) when they come home. It does not matter if they are gone for a few minutes, a few hours or days. We always greet them like we haven't seen them forever. We jump around making funny noises and can't wait for them to pet us. What is so cool is they seem as excited to see us as we are to see them. Pops and I have a special routine. He bends down with his arms extended toward me and calling for me. I run towards him with my head turned to the side, opening my mouth to show my teeth and making a growling noise. He knows that's my way of showing him how excited I am to see him. Guys just do things differently. You will see human guys with special handshakes, bro hugs or chest bumps. I guess males are just different, and Pops and me fit that category. This is just our way of being guys.

Being a Protective Brother

I TAKE MY RESPONSIBILITY AS AN older brother very seriously. For those of you that read my first book, you may remember I had a wonderful friend in Molly, my older sister. Molly taught me so many things which have helped me throughout my life. I experienced first-hand how an older sibling protects the younger one.

I have always put the utmost importance in protecting Heidi. I am there to always protect her from other dogs. Heidi tends to be like Mom in that she is a little verbal, but she knows I have her back. When we go to the boarding place when Mom and Pops go on vacation, I watch her closely, even if that means me sacrificing being able to make new friends or playing with the other dogs at playtime. Heidi tends to be more shy around other dogs and was not socialized as much when she was a pup. Therefore, I will always hang back with her to make sure she is safe and feels comfortable. It's just being the older brother.

When we go on walks, I will always pee on top of Heidi's pee so other dogs don't pick up on her scent. They need to know they will have to go through me to get to her. When she has come home from her surgeries, I will always try to comfort her. Sure, I will do the mandatory sniffing to see where she has been, but then I will try to make sure she is comfortable. Sometimes that just means giving her space and time to heal. Little sisters can be a pain.

There are times when I wish I had all the attention, like it was before Heidi joined the family. But overall, I would not trade for my time with Heidi. We have grown to become a pretty good team. We love each other, and we both know we have great peeps that love us deeply.

Happy Times

1. Anything with the entire family – walks, TV time, meals, etc.
2. The little things – going to get the mail out of the mailbox, weekend newspaper, yardwork.
3. Road trips – any excuse to go in the car, short or long trips. I always hunker down in the backseat. Years ago, I was riding in the car with Mom, and she slammed on the brakes which caused me to fly to the floorboard. After that incident, I have always been a little leery of riding too casual. I must admit I feel a little safer with Pops behind the wheel.
4. Dancing with Mom to *Doing It to Death* by Fred Wesley and the J.B.'s. She holds me tight as she sways to the music. I will lay my head on her shoulder, close my eyes and just cherish the moment. I don't know why that song became our signature song, but it did and I always love hearing it.
5. Being in bed with Mom and Pops before Pops would put Heidi and me in our room for the night. Sometimes, I would lay my head on Mom's pillow next to hers, and we would both snore. (Hers is louder than mine.) Sometimes, I

would take Pops' side before he came to bed. He and I would snuggle when he came to bed. Heidi would always go under the covers almost to the end of the bed. When Pops would tell us it was time to go to bed, she was always sound asleep, and he would drag her out from beneath the covers. He would say she was a "sack of potatoes," whatever that meant. Boy, we would enjoy that time together.

6. Another happy time was getting our special treat in the morning before Mom would leave. Mom or Pops would cut a special green treat in half and give half to me and half to Heidi. These treats were supposed to be good for our teeth. Dachshunds are notorious for having dental problems. I have had several teeth pulled because of decay. The lack of teeth has never slowed me down in chewing any type of food, certainly not these special treats which are very firm and need to be chewed extensively. I love it when Mom says, "Good treats for good pups." That was the signal for the best treat of the day.

7. Of course, playing ball. That is my favorite pastime. I especially like playing with Pops. He really knows how to "throw the rock." Mom, on the other hand, does not have the arm strength or accuracy Pops has. Pops told me she has a "rag arm" which I think he means affectionately that she can't throw. I could chase the ball for hours. I would sometimes take a break, catch my breath or get a shot of water and then get right back after it. Heidi never really cared for playing ball. She says, "What is the use? You chase the

ball, retrieve it, give it back and do it all over again." She thinks it is silly and a waste of energy. I love it.

8. Going to Pops' barbershop. As a long-haired dachshund, occasionally I get mats in my hair. Behind my ears or on my sides or legs, matted hair would develop. When Pops was petting me, he would run across the matted hair with his fingers. He would say, "Roo, we need to go to the barbershop." He would pick me up and carry me into his bathroom. He would set me up on the counter and carefully cut the matted hair out with his scissors. Once the trim was completed, Pops would slowly run his fingers through the hair of my entire body to make sure my hair was in perfect shape. I would think that final stage is what human guys get from their barbers with a massage or warm towel treatment. Dog, that felt good! Plus, I appreciated the matted area being gone. I felt freer in the wind, not having a balled-up area of hair holding me back. Heidi would get the same treatment from Pops except he would say, "Heidi, we need to go to the beauty parlor." Invariably, if one of us needed a hair treatment, the other would go and watch, knowing that Pops would give the onlooker as much attention as the first. He would always give the onlooker a rubdown and make a big fuss about how great he or she looked. When we were finished, we were looking good and feeling good.

9. Human food. There is something special about human food. Sure, I love my dry and canned food combination twice a day, but the chance to savor human food makes my mouth water. Some of my favorites are fish skin (trout or salmon), baked potato skin, broccoli, pizza bones (the crust part of the pizza), cheese, sardines, crackers, chips, watermelon (especially watermelon), and just about anything Mom and Pops will eat, I will eat.

Book Circuit

SOME OF YOU WILL remember my first book. Those of you that read it are probably much wiser due to all the lessons you learned from the book. If you did read it, I hope you enjoyed it. I really had a great time with what I call the book circuit. After the book was published, I was asked to make appearances with Pops and Mom.

If it was a school, children's time at a park or mall, Pops would read a chapter to the kids. I would sit next to him as he read my book. Once he would finish, the kids would clap, and I would start barking. It was my way of telling the kids I appreciated their applause.

When we were at a place where we sold the books, I would sit on the table where Pops would sign the books for me. I autographed the original for the publisher, but I was not about to dip my paw in ink every time someone wanted a copy of the book. I appreciate Pops filling in for me. Mom was our cashier. She either took credit card info or cash for each sale. Mom was also a great promoter of the book. She set up secure appearances through her connections. I loved everything about the book circuit. I enjoyed seeing the kids and watching them smile. I enjoyed being petted by young and old alike. I enjoyed posing for pictures with kids, families or adults that bought a book. One thing about me is you don't have to tell me to look into the camera or smile; I have it down. I must say that I am very photogenic. I must have gotten that from Mom because Pops doesn't like having his picture taken except when we take a picture together. I never see him smile as big as when we take a picture together. I guess it's that proud Papa theory. We even went to a senior living center as a stop on our circuit. Mom was working there at the time, and she set it up. It was really cool. Pops read a chapter, and then there was a question-and-answer period after the reading. While Pops handled the reading and the questions, I roamed the room getting pets, hugs and admiration from the seniors.

The whole book experience was great. You've heard of a "people person." Well, I am a "people dog." I love people and other dogs for that matter. I loved the attention, but I also enjoyed the time with my peeps. The only thing that would have made it better is if Heidi could have been there with us. However, Heidi is not a "people dog" or a "dog's dog." Plus, with Pops handling the reading and autographs, me working the room and Mom handling the cash, no one could have watched Heidi. Heidi really never got into the book anyway. She was very young when I wrote it, and she preferred to keep a lower profile.

Me Versus Crusoe

MOST DACHSHUND LOVERS have heard of Crusoe, the dachshund. He is an internationally-known dachshund blogger. His parents do a great job of promoting him and providing weekly updates on his life. Mom is a huge fan of Crusoe. She is always going on and on about the last Crusoe post. Pops, on the other hand, can't stand to hear about anything to do with Crusoe. He usually tells Mom something great about me or Heidi when she brings up a Crusoe comment. I admire what Crusoe and his parents have accomplished. They have brought a lot of attention to the doxie breed. Any dog that can bring notoriety to wiener dogs is alright with me. I know Pops is just prejudiced about his boy, but the way I look at it is this world is big enough for a superstar blogger like Crusoe and an author like me.

My Personality Traits

EVERYONE HAS THEIR OWN unique personality, and I am no different. It's funny how your personality can change under different circumstances. Take me and Heidi—we are as different as night and day. I am friendly to everyone, like other dogs and ready to play anytime. Heidi does not like strangers (will even snap at them), barks at kids and would rather lay around than play. However, when we go to the vet, Heidi is a perfect little angel. They talk about how sweet she is, doesn't bark and will let the doctor do whatever is needed without a whimper. Me, on the other hand, is a different story. I start trembling when I know we are going into the doctor's office. I shake so hard. I don't even want to see the other dogs.

I tend to squeal if the doctor comes close to me. Evidently, my actions have not gone unnoticed because the history chart with the doctor says "**Drama King**" in bold letters. I don't know why, but I can't seem to handle vet clinics. I don't know if it's the smells, hearing other dogs in other rooms or the fact that the doctor always wants to stick a thermometer up my rear end. It's just not a pleasant place. As soon as we leave, I go back to being Mr. Congeniality, and Heidi goes back to being the lonesome lover.

One thing I have noticed is that as I age, I have become more of a squealer. Whether I am running fast after a ball or someone picking me up unexpectantly, I let out a squeal. I was not always a squealer, but I definitely am now. I squeal so much that Pops calls me Dean Meminger. I had no idea who that was nor did Mom. Pop explained that Dean "The Dream" Meminger was a diminutive guard for the New York Knicks in the 70s. He did not have much of an outside shot so he would drive the lane with the ball and let out a squeal if someone touched him. Pop tends to be an expert on New York Knicks basketball. His favorite player growing up was Walt "Clyde" Frazier. Mr. Frazier's persona was always calm and cool under pressure. He would never change expressions, always under control. I guess that's where Pops got his coolness from Walt "Clyde" Frazier, and somehow, I got my squealing from Dean "The Dream" Meminger. I would have preferred for Pops to call me Dirk (Nowitzki) due to my German heritage. But two things were working against me on being called Dirk: (1) Dirk is 7 feet tall compared to my short doxie legs, and (2) Dirk was a grunter, not a squealer. Oh, well, I guess I will always be compared to Dean "The Dream."

Career

SOMETIMES IN LIFE, you think back about what you have accomplished and what you could have done. When I think about careers, I only have two mentors to examine, my peeps. Mom is affectionately called the butterfly by Pops. Mom has had numerous jobs in my lifetime. Just like a butterfly, she lands on a job, stays for a while and then flies off to her next destination. Her interests are varied or as Pops would say, "all over the map." There is nothing wrong with this approach. It is just very different from Pops. Pops has had two jobs his entire adult life. He worked for an engineering firm for 10 years after graduating from college and then started his own lighting com-

pany in 1986. Mom says Pops and I are a lot alike. We both are very structured and can set a watch by our actions. I think Heidi and Mom are very similar. They both have many interests, are very inquisitive, and their attitude is very carefree. They don't like structure like me and Pops; they just go with the flow. When I think about my life, I feel like I have packed a lot in, in a short time. I made it from Oklahoma to Texas when I was eight weeks old. I learned the dog ropes from a great mentor, Molly. She was a huge influence in my life. She taught me how to play, behave and have devotion to my peeps. My athletic skills were demonstrated at the Octoberfest Dachshund

Race when I was two years old. I came in second out of 120 entrants. I still say I would have won it if it had not been for a slow start out of the gate.

Then I wrote a book about *Life's Lessons*. As I mentioned earlier, I had a blast with the book circuit. The book changed my life because people noticed me, recognized me or made a fuss over me for years afterward.

So that's not a bad resume for a miniature long-haired dachshund. Sure, if I had won the dachshund race, I would have been tempted to represent all United States doxies in my homeland of Germany at their Octoberfest Dachshund Races. But who wants to deal with that 12-hour flight to Munich, applying for a passport and getting all the necessary shots for international travel. (I hate shots.)

Regarding the book, let's just say Oprah Winfrey read by book and wanted to recommend it to all her followers. I would have had to appear on one of her shows and be interviewed with Pops. I can just imagine all those women in the studio audience "ooing and aahhing" over me. Mom always had me wear a bowtie on our local book circuit. There is no telling what she would have me wear on national TV.

If I had a career change, I think it would be as a technician. I am always fascinated by the technicians that come to our house for service repairs. I normally bring a ball over to see if I can get them to throw the ball to me. Invariably, these technicians are too professional to be playing ball on the job. I quickly respect their commitment to their profession and watch intently as they work on our problem. Of all the technicians that have serviced our many homes, two have my utmost respect. Stevie is our HVAC technician, and he is the epitome of a professional. He always puts on his "booties" before entering the house, and he always looks crisp and sharp. Great HVAC technician, he really knows his stuff, and he keeps us comfortable year-round.

Jerry is the master electrician for Pops' company. Jerry has been with Pops since 1987. The neat thing about Jerry is he usually explains to me what he is doing and what he is finding. I would have liked to have been a technician like Stevie and Jerry, but a couple of things held me back. One, my paws do not grip tools that are necessary for the trade. I have been online to see if there are tools made for pups, but evidently there is not a strong demand. Secondly, I would not be able to wear a toolbelt. My tools would all fall out due to being a four-legged technician. I do think wearing a company shirt and cap would be cool. It certainly would make me look official.

Oh, well, it was just a dream.

You know, the more I think about it, I am very pleased with the way my life turned out just as it is. I am happiest when I am with my family. It would have been difficult for Heidi to make the trip to Germany or to see Oprah. I would much rather enjoy "family time" watching movies with my peeps and Heidi than being anywhere else.

Slowing Down

I GUESS IT IS INEVITABLE that we all slow down as we age. I thought Father Time would never catch me because I was too fast and youthful. Well, I am here to tell you no one gets a pass from Father Time.

I started to notice it when my arthritis started affecting my stamina. Mom, Heidi and I would go for walks around White Rock Lake with the "Price boys." Stanley and Oliver make up the "Price boys" with their mother Elise. For years, Stanley and Oliver would slow us down on walks because they were overweight. I liked leading the pack because I wanted to show everyone who the alpha dog was. We would go up to five-mile walks after having

to wait up for Stanley and Oliver. Mrs. Price started bringing a pet buggy so she could push Stanley and Oliver when they could not handle walking. Heidi also started needing a buggy due to her past back problem, so Mom bought a buggy for her. Much like Pops, I have a lot of pride, and I like to push myself to the limit. I would go the five miles all out, no matter the weather conditions, leading all the way.

Well, on some of our neighborhood family walks, Mom and Pops noticed I was really struggling. Pops started picking me up and carrying me home when we were halfway through our walk. At first, I was embarrassed that I couldn't physically handle the walks, but then

I was grateful Pops would carry me. It wasn't too much longer until I was confined to the buggy on the entire walk. Hey, I would much rather go for a ride and be with the family than being left at home. You can still smell all the scents and see all the sights from the buggy. It is not the same as being on the ground, but it will do. Many times, humans think Mom or Pops are pushing a human baby, only to see me, a long-haired dachshund, going for a ride. Heidi starts out walking around the neighborhood but quickly hitches a ride with me in the buggy. It's a tight fit, but we can manage.

My downfall began when my arthritis caused my right front leg to turn inwards. It was like a pronounced one-legged pigeon toe. My normal walk turned into a hobble. I started to think about doing simple tasks before doing it due to the severe pain even a few steps would cause. Eventually, my left hindleg would not support me. As I mentioned many times before, I loved playing ball with Pops. He could throw the ball as far as he could, and I would love chasing it down and returning it to him. We would do it for as long as the other could hold up. Usually, he would say, "One more, Roo," which meant we were going to shut it down. Dog, I loved those days! We had so much fun, and I think Pops was really proud of me, which was my goal all along. Sadly, it has come to the point where I can't run anymore. Instead of throwing the ball, Pops will roll the ball to me across the floor. Occasionally, he will slightly pitch it to me so I can catch it in midair. Pops makes a big deal out of my catch like the old days when I routinely would catch balls on the fly or off the bounce.

I know we can't do some things forever, but it is frustrating. My mind is reminding me of the past or telling me to run, but my body is not cooperating.

I am sleeping more, and when I am awake, I sit alone gazing out the window thinking of all the fun times we have had as a family. I know my peeps and Heidi know I am in pain. I see the looks in their eyes and not knowing how to best help me. Mom and Pops took me to the vet recently, and Dr. Thomas said that they needed to be thinking about the end. Even though I can't verbalize to them, I knew what she was talking about. I saw Mom and Pops break down in tears. I mustered all the strength I could and started walking around the exam room and giving them the best smile I could.

I think I fooled at least Pops because we went home and I played ball in the living room better than I had in months. Mom and Pops were so proud of me, and I loved every minute of it.

Even the thought of that has made me very tired. I am going to turn it over to Pops now. I trust him to tell you about the rest of my journey. I am just really, really tired....

Pops

THE LAST FEW MONTHS, Roo starting rapidly declining. We noticed that he was sleeping most of the day, not even getting up when we arrived. This was highly unusual because he loved greeting us and being at our sides constantly. When Annette and I were home together, Roo would stare out a window away from us. It became very painful for us to even watch him walk. He would try because he liked to please, but he moved very slowly.

Within the last couple of months, Roo would snap at you if you tried to touch him or squeal if you walked near him. That was not Roo's personality at all. On Friday, 9/1/23, Annette waited for me to get home to talk about the inevitable. Since she works from home, she would have a full day of watching his pain or constant sleeping. When I arrived, we discussed the situation, but I was reluctant to make a final decision on Roo's future.

Friday nights are pizza night, and we went to one of our favorite spots with the understanding we would continue to discuss. Shortly after our arrival, the General Manager, Drew, came over to talk to us. After a few minutes of small talk, Annette asked Drew what his wife did for a living. He said that she took calls for Lap of Love Veterinary Hospice. She answered calls from pet owners that needed to put their pets to sleep. Both of our mouths dropped open. We could not believe the coincidence and timing. This was one of the worst pizza nights Annette and I have shared. We could barely eat, thinking of the inevitable.

On Saturday, 9/2/23, Roo was worse. I came home about 1:00 p.m. from being at the office and working out. Annette suggested we call the vet. Our doctor was not available, and they would be closing at 2:00 p.m. Annette and I decided we did not want to take Roo to a clinic that he hated going to anyway. We preferred to have someone come to our home where he could remain as comfortable as possible and be with us. We decided to call Lap of Love after our conversation with Drew that night before. When I called, the person that answered my call was so calm and patient, especially since I could barely speak. The receptionist said that we would be receiving a call from the doctor between 3:00 p.m. and 5:00 p.m. to give us notice of when we should expect their arrival. I was able to sit with Roo for three hours before the doctor came. I took him outside which he loves. I carried him around, knowing this would be our last time together. I talked to him the entire time, telling him how much I loved him and how proud I was of him. I asked Annette to take pictures of us. Even though he was in so much pain, he still gave that Roo smile as she took several pictures.

Dr. Meg called at 3:45 p.m. and said she would arrive around 4:15 p.m. When she arrived, Roo would normally want to greet the person with a big smile and wagging tail. Today, he just sat on the couch without raising his head. Dr. Meg tried to touch Roo, and he snapped at her. This was so far from Roo's personality. Dr. Meg sat with us and observed Roo as Annette and I tried to explain to her his past few months. She noticed his odd breathing patterns. At times, it was very rapid like he had been running and then so slow you were not sure he was breathing.

Dr. Meg said Roo was experiencing allodynia which causes things that normally are not uncomfortable (like light touch or small muscle movements) to be painful. It develops when his body is working really hard to try to keep everything functioning and puts his body into a state that is similar to fight or flight. This happens most commonly with pets in the later stages of many diseases like cancer, kidney failure, heart failure, etc.

Dr. Meg said when we touched Roo, it would feel like needles going through his body. Dr. Meg gave him a medication she administered in his mouth to calm him down and take away the pain. After the medication, I was able to pet him and touch him like I had most of his life.

He seemed very peaceful with his eyes open as if he was aware of his surroundings.

Eventually, Annette and I told Dr. Meg we were prepared to say goodbye. When we asked Dr. Meg for some final time together, she left the room. After some tearful goodbyes, we asked Dr. Meg to return to the room. Dr. Meg administered the injection that put Roo to sleep.

During this entire process, Heidi was in the room where she sleeps. She never made a sound. It was as if she knew what was happening. We asked Dr. Meg if it would be appropriate to bring Heidi in to see Roo for a final time. She thought it would be good for closure. We put Heidi on the couch near Roo, and she turned her back to him as if she could not see him that way.

That Labor Day was the worst weekend I could ever remember. Annette, Heidi and I were extremely depressed. The home environment seemed so different, so empty.

Roo was the center of our universe, and now he was gone.

I personally was dealing with guilt and questioning whether we had done enough for Roo or given up too soon. Annette was constantly crying and wondering how she could go on without Roo's constant companionship. Heidi was extremely depressed. She would curl up behind the toilet in Annette's bathroom in the dark, go under our bed, or hide in the closet.

Annette and I will always remember the incredible sunset on Saturday, 9/2/23, in Dallas, Texas. (See photo)

When it had been 106 degrees without a cloud in the sky most of the summer, the sunsets had not been very different. The night Roo left us, the sunset was exceptional, so much so that a friend of Annette called to say it was Roo's signature goodbye.

Annette, Heidi and I are adjusting. Heidi no longer barks at other dogs on walks because Roo is not there to protect her. She is still very, very lonely, but she is adjusting. She gets 100% of the attention now, which she never really needed due to her independence.

Annette and I decided Heidi needs a companion. We can never replace Roo nor would we want to, but we do want to fill the void we are all experiencing.

In typical fashion, I began to thoroughly research the best dachshund breeder in North Texas. My research took me to one source. I called the recommended breeder who told me she just recently moved to North Carolina. I asked her if she could recommend a dachshund breeder in North Texas. She said there is only one breeder that she would recommend, and she gave me the information.

I called her recommendation and spoke with Amber. She recently had two litters which we could see from the pictures on her website. I told her

about our loss... and she said eight out of ten calls she receives are from pet owners that had recently lost their dog. I appreciated her patience and understanding. She seemed very knowledgeable about the breed and was very protective of her baby puppies. Annette and I made an appointment to drive to Gladewater in East Texas to see her puppies, in particular one named Rolo.

Rolo is a black, tan and white piebald long-haired miniature dachshund male. Annette and I fell in love with him at first sight. Rolo cuddled in our arms, never squirming or making a sound. We had brought Heidi along to see how she would respond to a puppy. She was very inquisitive but very cautious. By the way, Amber made sure Heidi had all of her vaccinations before she would allow us to bring her along. After a brief discussion, Annette and I decided to give Amber a down payment on the adoption of Rolo. He would not be ready to come home with us for another four weeks.

I was so impressed with Amber and the extra care she takes with her puppies. There is a viewing room with a small pen in the center. The puppies are placed in the pen for you to view. No one can wear shoes beyond the viewing room due to the germs that are carried on the bottom of shoes.

Amber explained Rolo will have one vaccination and a vet report when we pick him up. He will get his second vaccination after a certain number of weeks which she described in paperwork she will provide us.

I asked her when we should have Rolo neutered. She says it varies, and it is determined when male dogs begin to raise their legs to pee. She said if a dog is neutered too early, it can cause severe arthritis. My heart just sank. Roo had been neutered when we picked him up at eight weeks. It made me sick that he was doomed from such an early age by an inexperienced breeder.

There is nothing we can do about that now. We just hope that Roo knew how much we loved him. I have told Annette that I am big on certain signs in life that I don't think happen by accident. There have been certain occasions in my life that I believe were signs or messages from God. Annette is the most spiritual person I know. I asked her if she believes our pets will be in heaven. She believes pets have souls and that God takes care of those with a soul. Roo most definitely had a soul. All you had to do was to look at those expressive eyes of his and you would know there was great depth to his soul.

My hope is that when I leave this earth and make it to the Pearly Gates, I will be accepted for fighting the good fight. Once I enter, I hope to see Roo with a ball in his mouth waiting for me. Hopefully, he will drop the ball, start running towards me with his head tilted slightly, showing his teeth as he leaps into my arms. At that point, he will say, "Pops, you are going to love it here. Let's go play!"

Roo, this book was written as a tribute to you.

I miss you, buddy!

Pops

P.S. I think the name Rolo is short for Roo love.

www.ingramcontent.com/pod-product-compliance
Lightning Source LLC
Chambersburg PA
CBHW060944100426

42813CB00016B/2860